IMAGES
of America

FORT LEE

"THE SONG OF CAMP LEE." In April 1917, the communities of Petersburg and Hopewell, Virginia, learned that the Army would build a 5,300-acre cantonment located between the two cities to be named Camp Lee in honor of Confederate General Robert E. Lee. Sixty days were given to build the camp. It was expected to cost over $11 million, and would house and train 40,000 soldiers. Although never destined to achieve the fame as "Over There" and "Yankee Doodle Dandy," this locally written music expressed the patriotic enthusiasm of the local residents and soldiers training at Camp Lee during World War I.

Tim O'Gorman and Dr. Steve Anders

ISBN 978-0-7385-1524-3

Published by Arcadia Publishing,
Charleston, South Carolina

Printed in the United States of America.

Library of Congress Catalog Card Number: 2003102278

For all general information contact Arcadia Publishing at:
Telephone 843-853-2070
Fax 843-853-0044
E-Mail sales@arcadiapublishing.com
For customer service and orders:
Toll-Free 1-888-313-2665

Visit us on the Internet at www.arcadiapublishing.com

QUARTERMASTER REGIMENT CEREMONY, 1986. The Army's Quartermaster Corps dates from June 16, 1775, when the Continental Congress authorized the position of the Quartermaster General. In World War II, the Quartermaster School was established at Camp Lee and since 1962, Fort Lee has been known as the "Home of the Quartermaster Corps." Quartermasters provide a variety of logistical support including supply, subsistence, mortuary services, petroleum and water, field laundry and bath, aerial delivery, and parachute packing. In 1986, the "Quartermaster Regiment" was established as part of the Army's Regimental System. Presenting the Regimental colors to Maj. Gen. Eugene Stillions, the Quartermaster General, is Gen. Richard H. Thompson, Commander, United States Army Material Command, assisted by Command Sgt. Maj. Rosvelt Martain. General Thompson's career took him from a Private First Class to the rank of four-star General, making him the highest-ranking Quartermaster General Officer in the Corps's history.

Contents

ACKNOWLEDGMENTS

The authors have many people to thank for their support and encouragement during the writing of *Fort Lee*. Foremost is the Command Group of the United States Army Quartermaster Center and School, including Maj. Gen. Terry E. Juskowiak, our 47th Quartermaster General and Commander of Fort Lee; Brig. Gen. Scott G. West, Deputy Commander of Fort Lee; and our immediate boss, Col. Douglas Glover, Chief, Office of the Quartermaster General.

Active participation and inspiration came from members of the Army Quartermaster Foundation, former Quartermasters who during their careers made much of the history that we have written about and who now work to perpetuate the heritage of the Quartermaster Corps. Their ranks include Maj. Gen. (retired) Eugene Stillions, the 39th Quartermaster General, Maj. Gen. (retired) Joseph Pieklik, and Col. (retired) Robert Barrett.

We owe special thanks to Dr. Peter Skirbunt, Public Affairs Officer at the Defense Commissary Agency and to Ms. Peggy Payne, Army Logistics Management College, for the loan of photographs of those organizations. And to Chris Calkins, Jimmy Blankenship, Grant Gates, and Robin Snyder at nearby Petersburg National Battlefield for material on Petersburg and Hopewell in the Civil War.

A particular thank you also goes to Luther Hanson, Museum Specialist, co-worker, and keeper of the archives at the Quartermaster Museum, for his expertise and help in locating images from the vast collection of the museum.

But most of all, the authors acknowledge their debt to the selfless service of the thousands of Army Quartermasters, past and present, who have made Fort Lee's story worth telling.

INTRODUCTION

The story of Fort Lee is about a place, people, and the United States Army Quartermaster Corps. It is the story of a changing 20th-century army and its transition to the 21st. It is the story of neighboring communities—military and civilian—that share the immediate impact of world events. And it is the story of thousands of men and women who through the years have entered Fort Lee as civilians and left as soldiers.

The story begins on a June day in 1917 when land was cleared outside of Petersburg, Virginia, to build a National Army Cantonment called Camp Lee. America had just entered World War I and for citizens of nearby Petersburg and Hopewell the arrival of the Army was welcome news. The Camp would become a source of civic pride and economic well-being.

Camp Lee was unique because it was built on the ground where the Battle of Petersburg was fought 52 years earlier. As young men from Virginia, Pennsylvania, and West Virginia arrived to form the 80th Division and to train together, the symbolism was not lost on area residents. Camp Lee was to help the healing of sectional wounds in a way that rhetoric and patriotic gestures never could.

With a population of over 60,000, Camp Lee soon became the third largest "city" in Virginia, behind Richmond and Norfolk. The 80th Division departed for France and was replaced by the 37th Division, but before they finished training the war ended. Less than a year later Camp Lee was dismantled, a portion of the land going to Petersburg National Battlefield, and the rest used to create a Virginia state game preserve.

By 1940 Europe was again at war, and America had begun to remobilize. Several of the old World War I camps and cantonments were reactivated, and everywhere, it seemed, a building frenzy was underway. By October of that year a second Camp Lee had emerged from the Virginia farmlands on the same ground as the original, as the site for the Quartermaster Corps Replacement Training Center. The Quartermaster Corps is the Army branch that provides supplies and services, such as laundry and bath, graves registration, clothing, fuel, and food to combat troops in the field.

A new Quartermaster "Center" was activated at Camp Lee in February 1941, and by October the Quartermaster School had also been relocated from Philadelphia. During World War II, more than 300,000 Quartermaster officers and soldiers were trained at Camp Lee. They formed units ranging from depot battalions to grave registration companies, and performed such diverse tasks as cooking, packing mules, and repairing shoes. Camp Lee–trained Quartermaster officers commanded these units, and also helped plan logistics for major operations from the

South Pacific campaigns to D-Day. One Camp Lee Quartermaster, Pvt. George Watson, was awarded the Medal of Honor. The performance of Quartermasters during the war forcefully demonstrated the importance of trained logisticians. So when the war ended, Camp Lee remained operational.

In 1948, the Women's Army Corps (WAC) Training Center arrived. WACs had served with distinction during World War II, and as a result were granted permanent status through passage of the Women's Armed Services Integration Act in 1948. The WAC Training Center remained at Fort Lee until 1954, when it was moved to Fort McClellan, Alabama.

In 1950, Camp Lee became "Fort Lee" when the Army decided to permanently retain the post. The Korean War, and the Cold War that followed, touched Fort Lee directly and, in turn, Fort Lee contributed to the fight. The installation trained Quartermasters for service in Korea, in Europe at outposts along the Iron Curtain, and later in Vietnam. In 1950, Quartermasters took on the Army's aerial delivery and parachute-packing mission, and a new Parachute Rigger School was opened at Fort Lee. During the course of the decade, other functions that had been carried out elsewhere in the country, such as subsistence and petroleum operations training, were consolidated there. A four-story reinforced bunker was built, containing a component of the Washington, D.C. air defense sector, which provided a constant reminder of Cold War tensions. And families arrived. By the mid-1950s, on-post housing became available for officers and non-commissioned officers and their families.

Although officially called the "Home of the Quartermaster Corps" since 1962, by the end of the 20th century Fort Lee was also home to other organizations, including the Army Logistics Management College, an institution of higher learning for logisticians, and the Defense Commissary Agency, the organization that operates nearly 300 Armed Forces Commissaries throughout the world. The overall command of Fort Lee resides with the Combined Arms Support Command, the organization that develops doctrine and future combat systems for all the Army logistics branches.

But the main activity at Fort Lee remains training Quartermasters, over 25,000 of them each year. And like the thousands of Fort Lee-trained Quartermasters before them, these soldiers leave for service worldwide. This is, perhaps, Fort Lee's most significant story—the story of a rite of passage in young lives; the story of a transformation from civilians to soldiers. For many, it was the most pivotal event of their lives and many return to Fort Lee to relive it.

Veterans of World War II, Korea, Vietnam, and the Gulf War come daily to visit the place where their lives were changed forever. They drive the roads with their families looking for familiar places. But what they see is change. The wooden barracks are gone, and brick and concrete buildings sit on fields where they once drilled. WAC veterans see only an empty field where their training center once stood. But they also see young men and women learning to be soldiers and undergoing their own rite of passage.

Fort Lee's story is thus a continuing one. As the place that holds the collective memories of the thousands who once served here, it is also the place where memories continue to be made for those who live, work, and train at Fort Lee, the Home of the Quartermaster Corps.

One

IN VIRGINIA'S HISTORIC HEARTLAND

UNION MORTAR, "THE DICTATOR," OUTSIDE PETERSBURG, 1864. Today's Fort Lee is located in central Virginia, south of Richmond, and not far from several antebellum plantations along the James River, Jamestown, and Colonial Williamsburg—in the Old Dominion's historic heartland. On the very same ground where Revolutionary War and Civil War armies once fought, and some of our country's greatest leaders (including President Lincoln) once stood, Fort Lee now stands.

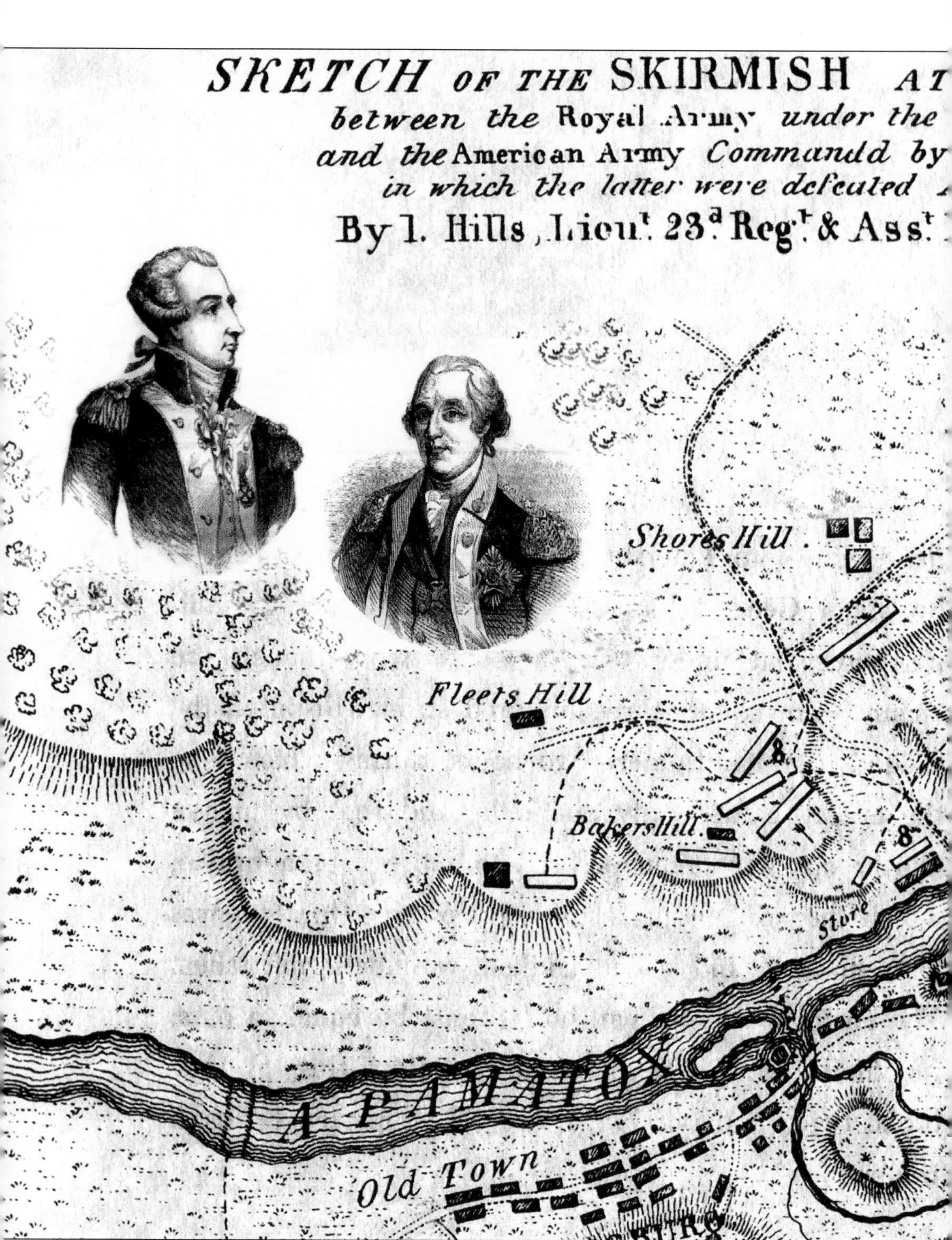

BATTLE OF PETERSBURG, APRIL 25, 1781. A group of some 2,500 British regulars landed on the banks of the James River, marched across present-day Fort Lee, and attacked a much smaller force of American militiamen defending Petersburg. The militia, under Gen. von Steuben

(right inset), held for three precious hours before retreating. This allowed time enough for Major General Lafayette (left inset) and his Continentals to move in and keep the capital city of Richmond from falling.

PETERSBURG, VIRGINIA, IN THE CIVIL WAR, 1864–1865. Petersburg on the eve of the Civil War had a population of just over 18,000—which included one of the largest free black populations anywhere in the South—and was among the top 50 most industrialized cities in the country. Strategically located on the south bank of the Appomattox River, 23 miles south of the Confederate capital of Richmond, it served as a major road and rail center throughout the war. Five railroads converged on this spot, and from them military supplies were forwarded to Gen. Robert E. Lee's Army of Northern Virginia. In the last year of the war, a combined Union force of over 100,000 troops attacked Petersburg hoping to cut off Richmond from its supply base. The nine-and-a-half month siege that followed was the longest in American history.

GRANT (LEFT) VERSUS LEE (RIGHT), THE SIEGE OF PETERSBURG, 1864–1865. Confederate General Lee's outnumbered troops at Petersburg were well protected behind a 10-mile chain of breastworks and artillery emplacements known as the "Dimmock Line," named after the engineer who designed it, Capt. Charles H. Dimmock. A thin woodline today separates Fort Lee from surviving remnants of those same Union and Confederate trenches.

Battle of the Crater, July 30, 1864. In an effort to end the siege of Petersburg in "one fell swoop," members of the Union 48th Pennsylvania Regiment came up with the idea of digging a mine under the heavily fortified Confederate works. It took nearly a month to complete the tunnel and pack it with more than four tons of black powder explosives. The explosion in the pre-dawn hours of July 30th killed some 278 Confederate soldiers, and left a gaping crater over 170 feet long and 80 feet wide—through which hundreds of Yankees soon poured. But a prompt response by the defenders prevented a breakthrough, and led to a major disaster for the North.

UNITED STATES MILITARY RAILROAD. During the summer and fall of 1864, the Union Army built a railroad to carry supplies along the Federal lines besieging Petersburg. Beginning at the Army supply depot in City Point (below) and ultimately extending more than 20 miles, it was the longest military railroad built during the Civil War. The railroad traversed present-day Fort Lee where one of the stops included Meade's Station, near the headquarters of the Commander of the Army of the Potomac, Gen. George Meade (right).

AFRICAN AMERICANS AT CITY POINT DEPOT, 1864. The Union supply depot at City Point, Virginia (present-day Hopewell, less than five miles from Fort Lee) was one of the busiest ports in the world during the last year of the Civil War. Hundreds of former slaves worked on the docks as stevedores, and served as cooks, bakers, hospital attendants, and laborers of every sort.

UNION WAGONS PASS THROUGH PETERSBURG, 1865. The siege ended on April 2, 1865. General Grant's long columns moved through the abandoned city in an effort to catch up with Lee's retreating army. Appomattox was but a week away.

Two

Camp Lee National Army Cantonment

Camp Lee Doughboy. Built in the summer of 1917 upon America's entry into World War I, Camp Lee was the training site for the 80th Division recruited from Virginia, West Virginia, and Pennsylvania. When the Division left for France in May 1918, it was replaced by the 37th Division. Among the over 60,000 soldiers who trained at Camp Lee was this unidentified soldier who probably had this studio portrait taken to send home as a memory of his Army experience, a practice first widely seen in the Civil War and continuing today.

ROAD CONSTRUCTION, 1917. Construction of Camp Lee began June 10, 1917. In a little over three months more than 1,500 buildings and 15 miles of road were completed; at the peak of construction over 13,000 workers were onsite. It was built on a portion of Petersburg Battlefield, and cannon balls, shells, and bullets from that battle were dug up during construction.

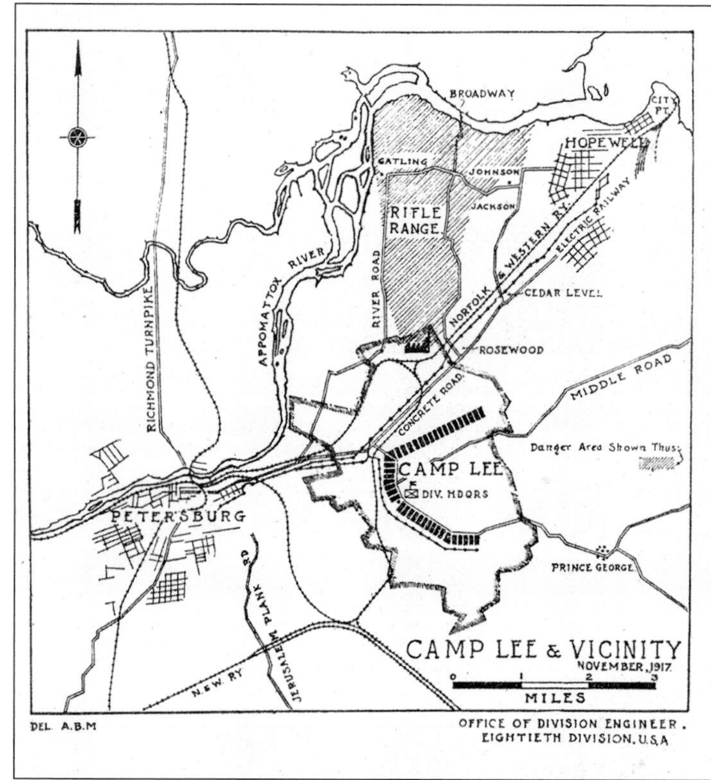

CAMP LEE MAP, 1917. Camp Lee was one of the 32 National Army Cantonments and National Guard Camps established at the outset of World War I. Laid out in the shape of a horseshoe, the camp stretched two miles from tip to tip.

THE 80TH DIVISION HEADQUARTERS. The first soldiers trained at Camp Lee were members of the 80th Division, whose ranks included recruits from Virginia, West Virginia, and Pennsylvania. The division was organized at Camp Lee on August 5, 1917 and underwent training and conditioning for the next nine months before embarking for France in May 1918. While at Camp Lee, the "Davis House" (the white house above) served as the Divisional Headquarters for its commander, Maj. Gen. Adelbert Cronkhite (right).

Panoramic Photograph of Camp Lee, 1917. Pvt. Hugh Donaldson, a soldier training at Camp Lee in July 1918, wrote home to say: "This camp is laid out in the shape of a horse shoe and it would take you a day or more to walk around it where we drill. They used to raise peanuts

Company Areas. Soldiers were housed with their Company in designated areas and were responsible for keeping their areas neat and clean. This view of a Company area, probably taken from the fire watch tower across from the Divisional Headquarters, provides a closer look at the layout of Company "streets" and shows how well the areas were maintained.

and that is about all could be raised for there is nothing but sand here. You could not find a stone here to throw at a dog." This view was taken from the camp's water tower that stood between A and B Avenues in the vicinity of 27th Street.

INFANTRY BARRACKS. Soldiers of the 80th Division were housed in the Army's standard 200-man barracks. When the first recruits began to arrive in September 1917, construction was still underway.

RECRUITS ARRIVING AT CAMP LEE, AUGUST 1917. When America entered World War I, the nation was swept by patriotism and young men—including many from the local area—rushed to join up for the chance to fight the "Bosch."

NEW RECRUITS, SEPTEMBER 1917. World War I was the largest mobilization of the Army since the Civil War. It was also America's first modern war, fought with tanks, vehicles, airplanes, and submarines. The urgency to send American forces to Europe was tempered by the need to properly train the new Army for the rigors of trench warfare. Young recruits had to be transformed quickly from enthusiastic civilians into competent soldiers.

RECENTLY VACCINATED RECRUITS. All soldiers entering the Army were vaccinated against typhoid, a practice that the Army had made mandatory by 1911.

DRILLING WITH STICKS. Fresh recruits, with one not yet in uniform (center), practice drills with wooden sticks rather than weapons. Until supplies of weapons and equipment arrived, instructors had to make do with substitutes. Constant drills emphasized teamwork and taught soldiers to respond quickly to orders.

WEAPONS TRAINING. Firing practice was conducted on nearby ranges. Marching and weapons training were frequent training activities at Camp Lee. Above, recruits learn the manual of arms while those below are learning squad tactics.

Doughboy Snapshot, Camp Lee, 1918. This snapshot of an unidentified soldier was taken at Camp Lee's trench warfare training site. This elaborate trench system was constructed to familiarize soldiers with what they would encounter in France. After arriving in France, soldiers received additional training in trench warfare before being posted along the front.

Machine Gun Training. The machinegun would prove to be the most lethal weapon of World War I. Despite the casual pose of the soldiers in this postcard photograph, learning to use—and avoid—machine guns was important.

INTERIOR OF MESS HALL, 1918. While not often known for its quality, Army food was available in enough quantity and nutritional value to make the American soldier the best fed in the world. For many soldiers from poorer areas, the Army provided the best food they had ever had.

CAMP LEE COOKS, 1917. The Army's first school for cooks was held at Fort Riley in 1905. By 1917, the Quartermaster Corps was responsible for providing and preparing the food for the Army.

CAMP LEE BANDS, 1918. Music played an important role in the life of Camp Lee. Each Regiment had a band, such as the 62nd Infantry Regiment (above) and the Base Hospital (below). Bands provided the music for parades and reviews, and played concerts for soldiers and the local community, a tradition that continues to this day.

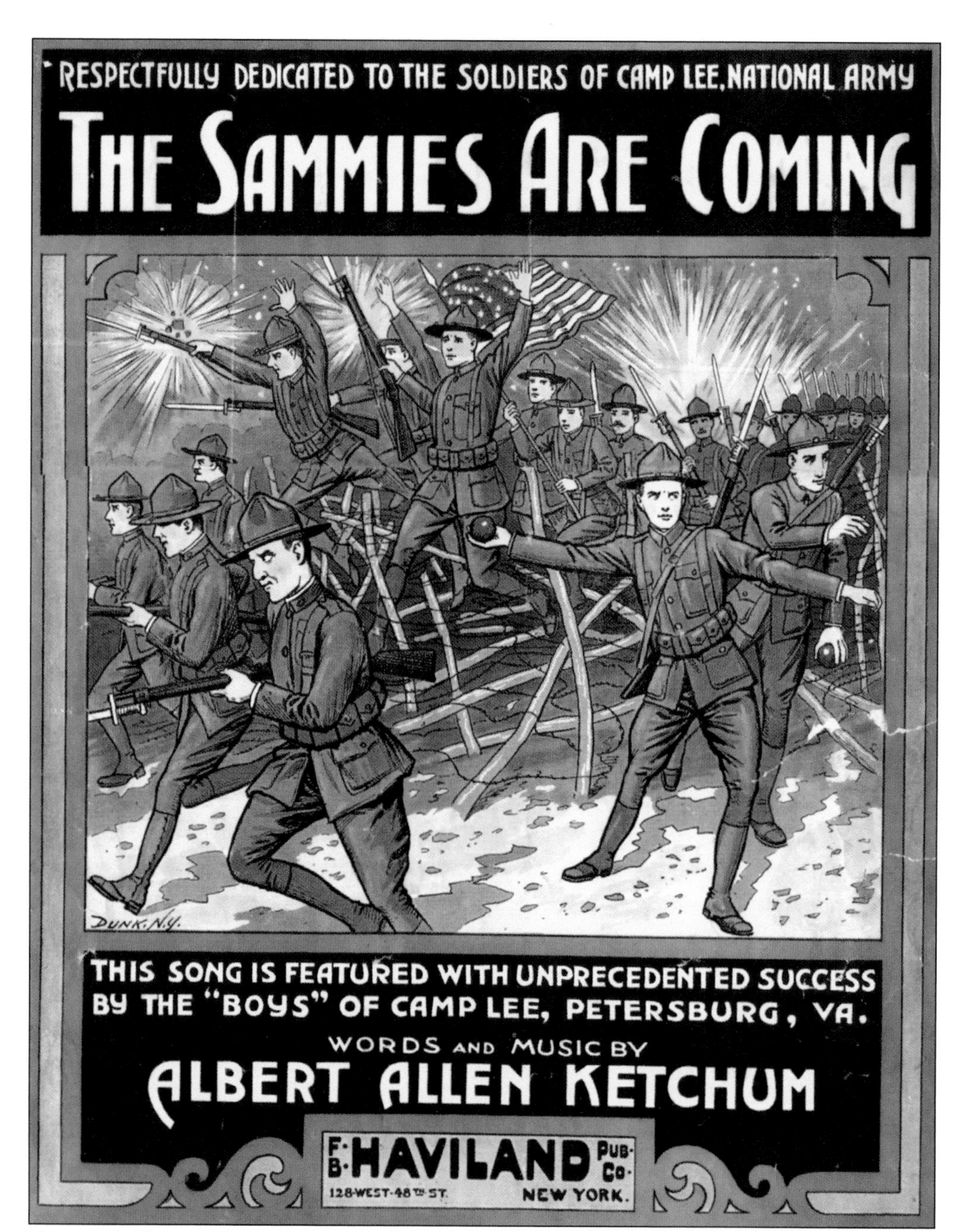

PATRIOTIC PARLOR SHEET MUSIC. Before radio and television, mass entertainment was confined largely to music either listened to in concerts or played in the home. World War I provided a market for new music and publishers were quick to meet the demand with new patriotic music. Although "Sammies" (in the song title above) was a nickname used for American soldiers during World War I, the more common and popular term was "Doughboys."

MAKING A PANORAMIC PHOTOGRAPH, 329TH TRUCK COMPANY, CAMP LEE. Panoramic photographs were a popular method at the time for capturing large groups of people and wide scenes. This photographer is getting ready to make a panoramic portrait of officers and men of the 329th Truck Company, stationed at Camp Lee in 1918, and located approximately where the Petersburg National Battlefield Park Visitor Center is located today.

BLACK SOLDIERS, 1918. More than 400,000 African Americans served in World War I, including those (above) assigned to Camp Lee. The majority of black soldiers were in the Services of Supply (SOS), in Quartermaster, stevedore, and pioneer infantry units—virtually all of them segregated.

CAMP LEE HOSPITAL. Included among the facilities at Camp Lee was its hospital. Sitting on 52 acres, the hospital served not only the soldiers in training but also received wounded soldiers returned from Europe. Perhaps the most trying time for the hospital and its staff (below) was the nation-wide flu epidemic in the of winter 1918. At Camp Lee, an estimated 10,000 soldiers were stricken by the flu. Over 500 died in the course of a few weeks.

FIRE STATION NO. 1. Fire was a constant concern in a community of 40,000 living in buildings made entirely of wood. Camp Lee had three fire stations, run by the Quartermaster Corps. In addition, each soldier in the barracks would be assigned fire guard duty.

HOSTESS HOUSE. The Hostess House, located directly across from the Headquarters building, was operated by the YWCA and served as a suitable meeting place for soldiers and their visiting mothers, sisters, and girlfriends. The House was operated by YWCA hostesses who served not only as attendants but as chaperones as well.

Hostess House Employee (right) and the Inside of the Hostess House (below). Most of the employees of the Hostess House were from the local communities. A camp guide written at the time described the Hostess House like this: "The workers, representatives of the YWCA, give them [the visitors] a cordial welcome, and do everything possible for their comfort. The house has a lounging room, writing-rooms, a cafeteria, and files of current magazines, musical instruments, and many other conveniences are at the disposal of the guest."

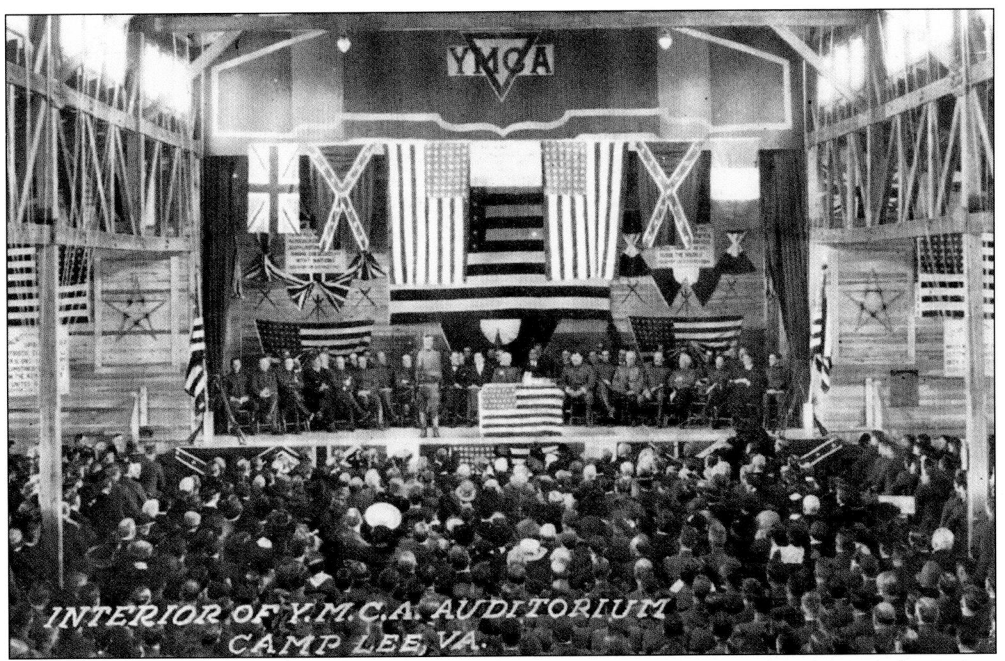

YMCA AUDITORIUM. In 1918, a soldier wrote his sister to assure her that he was doing fine at Camp Lee: "You can get all the writing paper and envelopes you want at the Knights of Columbus or the YMCA and all the time there is something going on at the YMCA. You can see some good moving picture shows and some boxing and it is all free for uncles' boys."

KNIGHTS OF COLUMBUS HALL, CAMP LEE. The Knights of Columbus operated halls as a service to soldiers. Although a Catholic organization, the sign "Everybody Welcome" indicates that all faiths were encouraged to visit. The halls provided reading rooms, writing materials, and places to relax away from the stress of Army training.

THE DAVIS HOUSE, RESIDENCE OF THE COMMANDING GENERAL. When the land for Camp Lee was acquired by the Army, a farmhouse stood on the property. The house served as the Headquarters for the 80th Division and later as the residence of the Division Commander, Maj. Gen. Adelbert Cronkhite. After the war, the house was purchased by the Davis family and was incorporated into the second Camp Lee during World War II. Today the house serves as a VIP quarters and is the oldest building on the post.

UNIDENTIFIED COUPLE, 1918. Camp Lee during World War I also had a domestic side. Families of soldiers stationed permanently at Camp Lee could live nearby. The Camp also had a school (below) for the children of the permanent staff.

Infantry Replacement Company, 1918. After the 80th Division left Camp Lee in May 1918, the 37th Division arrived for training. Camp Lee continued to serve as a training center for replacements being sent to France.

Soldier Parade in Petersburg, 1918. Petersburg citizens felt particularly proud of Camp Lee. Local civic groups and organizations provided amenities and recreation for soldiers both on and off post. The Army responded with patriotic parades for the citizens of Petersburg such as the one above.

Pvt. Apel Vartanian, 1917. There were many local citizens who trained at Camp Lee. Among them was Apel Vartanian of Hopewell. This image is an artist's colorized version of a snapshot taken of Vartanian while stationed at Camp Lee.

Pvt. Fred Priode, 1917. Fred Priode, born in the Virginia mining town of Clintwood as the oldest of 13 children, enlisted in the Army and was trained as a Wagoner at Camp Lee. He went overseas with the 80th Division and on October 7, 1918, was killed in action during the Argonne Offensive. The death benefit sent to his parents was used by them to send their remaining children to college, including one of Fred's sisters, June Hawks of neighboring Prince George, Virginia.

LIVING UNCLE SAM, CAMP LEE, 1919. On 13 January 1919, artist-photographer Arthur S. Mole and his partner, John D. Thomas, took this "living" photograph of Uncle Sam composed of 19,000 soldiers and officers at Camp Lee. During and after World War I, such living photographs were popular and Mole was one of the best practitioners. Soldiers made good subjects. Unlike civilians, they could be directed to stand for the hours it took to pose and shoot the photograph, and they didn't need to be paid for their time.

Three

Camp Lee Reborn in World War II

Fourth Quartermaster School Regiment, Camp Lee, 1943. The Quartermaster Replacement Training Center was opened at Camp Lee in February 1941. Within months the number of trainees and permanent party exceeded 30,000, with more arriving every day. Training was done in regimental units on a 13-week schedule, later shortened to 8 weeks, and divided between basic and technical courses of instruction. Their guiding maxim: "Soldier first, Quartermaster technician second."

REBUILDING CAMP LEE, VIRGINIA, 1941. In October 1940, at the height of the emergency mobilization period preceding Pearl Harbor, the War Department issued orders for the construction of a second Camp Lee on the same site as the original cantonment. Like its predecessor it was laid out in a U-shaped pattern, extending nearly four miles from tip to tip. The first troops to arrive lived in tents, as hundreds of construction works, plumbers, electricians, and others went about building barracks, mess halls, classrooms, and the countless other facilities needed to train those about to embark in global warfare.

NEWLY DESIGNED BARRACKS, QUARTERMASTER SCHOOL, 1941. In the hectic months leading up to the United States's entry into World War II, military planners unveiled architectural designs and began constructing by the thousands the new 700 series, 63-man barracks. With its indoor shower room, sinks and latrine, unpainted walls, and bare studs, this "unlovely and unloved" abode stood at the heart of soldier life at Camp Lee as elsewhere. Quickly and easily constructed, a new barracks was estimated to be going up at the rate of one every 54 minutes at some installations.

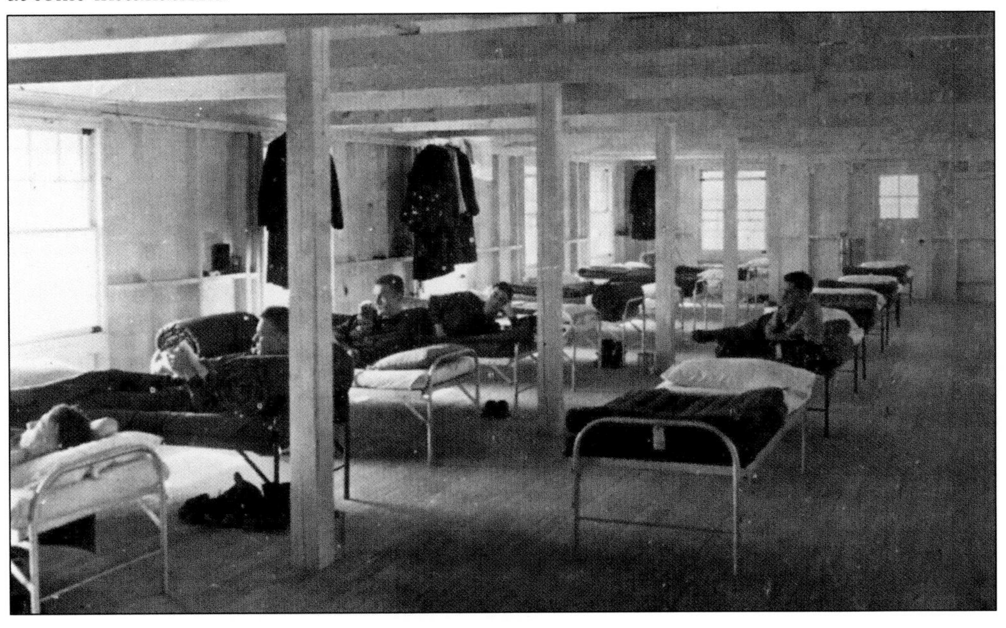

MAJ. GEN. JAMES E. EDMONDS, CAMP LEE COMMANDER, 1941. General Edmonds, a National Guard officer and World War I veteran, was recalled to active duty during the emergency period. A well-known newspaper writer and editor before the war, he became an NBC radio commentator after his retirement from active duty in December 1943. He is pictured here astride his favorite mount, "El Duro."

PANORAMA OF CAMP LEE, VIRGINIA, 1944. Spread across hundreds of acres in the piney woods of south central Virginia, Camp Lee became the home of the Quartermaster Replacement Training Center, the Quartermaster School, Army Service Forces Headquarters,

MAIN INTERSECTION, CAMP LEE, VIRGINIA, 1944. Here a military police officer assists a new recruit looking for the Post Reception Center.

a Women's Army Corps detachment, a 1,000-bed Regional Hospital, a major Army Reception Center, and even a prisoner of war camp.

RECRUIT RECEPTION CENTER, CAMP LEE, 1942. New recruits heading back to their barracks after a trip to the Supply Section to pick up their uniforms are seen here. By June 1942, the number of selectees entering the Quartermaster Corps outnumbered volunteers two to one. All new men were tested and interviewed, classified and assigned on the basis of prewar occupational skills, and physical and intellectual capacity.

Basic Military Training, Camp Lee, 1942. Following the registration process, new recruits were introduced to military discipline and courtesy, and instructed in such things as drill and ceremony, first aid, military sanitation and sex hygiene, and care of clothing and equipment.

THE SOLDIER'S LIFE. Whether in the barracks or on bivouac, the more seasoned drill sergeants and noncommissioned officers served as front line trainers, mentors, and disciplinarians for raw recruits.

DIGGING FOXHOLES. Training of enlisted soldiers was meant to make them physically fit, indoctrinate them in Army ways, emphasize the importance of teamwork, and teach them how to take care of themselves in the field.

WEAPONS TRAINING AND MAINTENANCE. All service of supply soldiers sent to Camp Lee for basic and advanced training were required to become familiar with the .30 caliber M1 rifle.

RIFLE PRACTICE, QUARTERMASTER REPLACEMENT TRAINING CENTER, 1941. Quartermaster trainees received in-class training on the theory of good marksmanship, followed by several days of close supervision on the rifle range.

Physical Training. At least a half-hour's time of the soldier's daily training routine was devoted to calisthenics. Approved exercises designed to make the trainee fit, and help to him retain that well-proportioned figure, started off each day.

Obstacle Courses. Seven feet of wall were nothing to these hearty troops who swarmed over it with the aid of ropes and blocks in the obstacle course race that comprised part of the physical training of Quartermaster troops at Camp Lee.

CARGO LOADING NETS, 1944. Every soldier at Camp Lee had to learn the correct method of debarking from large vessels into small boats for amphibious operations. Here, while wearing gas masks and carrying rifles, trainees swarm down the rope nets used as ladders while smoke, furnished by the Camp Chemical Warfare Section, swirls about the tower.

OBSTACLE COURSE AT LAKE JORDAN. The Quartermaster School built a new obstacle course and amphibious warfare training center at Lake Jordan, south of Petersburg, in the summer of 1943. The lake also served as a recreational facility, with boating, fishing, swimming, and also a small clubhouse and dance pavilion.

CHEMICAL WARFARE SECTION, CAMP LEE, 1943. Selected officers and noncommissioned officers at the Quartermaster School received intensive training in chemical warfare, so as not to be caught unprepared in the event of German gas attacks.

"U.S. TROOPS CAPTURE NAZI GESTAPO HEADQUARTERS." This might have been the caption for this picture taken of the 13th Quartermaster Training Regiment during a demonstration of the principles of urban warfare. After the demonstration, the "ghost" of each man who "died" told student observers the mistake he had made.

FIRST QUARTERMASTER DEMONSTRATION BATTALION, CAMP LEE, 1944. Here a light maintenance company lined up for inspection shows Quartermaster School officer candidates the vehicles and tools needed to quickly transport infantry troops into battle areas.

TANK DEFENSE TAUGHT AT THE QM SCHOOL. Trainees learned how to dig foxholes and crouch in them while machinegun-toting armored vehicles churned overhead. They also learned how to toss "Molotov Cocktails" and hand grenades at these "steel monsters."

CAMP LEE BAKERY TRUCK. With an average population of more than 30,000 soldiers, the installation had its own bakery, commissary store, wholesale laundry and dry cleaning plant, and other facilities needed to sustain a medium-sized "city."

PULLING KP. Scrubbing up after serving a meal in the field are these students at the Cooks and Mess Sergeants School at Camp Lee.

BAND TRAINING UNIT, CAMP LEE, 1943. Band trainees at the Quartermaster Replacement Training Center receive instruction in the correct twist of the "stick." Learning to use the baton in a snappy military manner was part of their specialized training in the unit.

DRUM AND BUGLE CORPS, 6TH QM TRAINING REGIMENT, CAMP LEE. The regimental band's purpose was to lend musical support for parades, official ceremonies, and other special events. They also entertained audiences with march music, light overtures, and popular tunes.

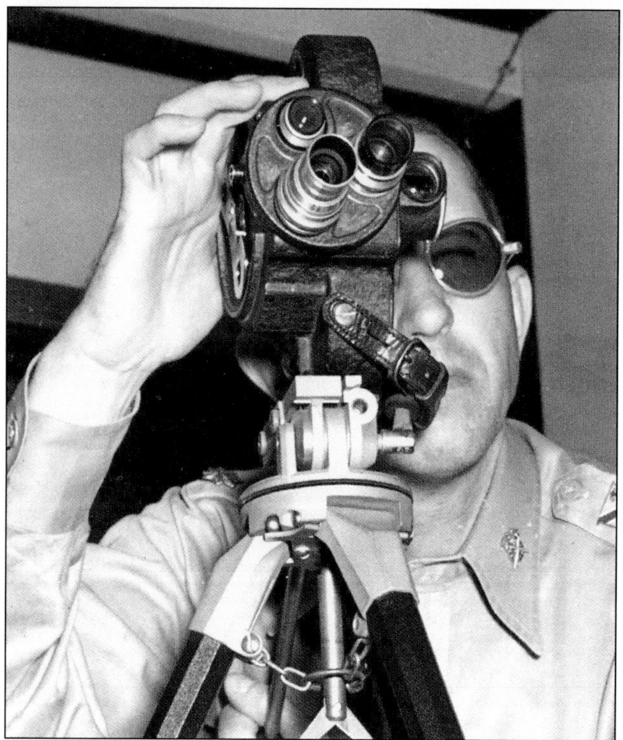

TYPICAL CLASSROOM SCENE IN A TYPIST COURSE. The Technical Service Section of the Quartermaster School produced a large array of models, graphic illustrations, sand table exhibits, and other training aids to help with the teaching of technical courses. The training aid shown here is an electrically controlled typewriter keyboard.

TRAINING FILM PRODUCTION, CAMP LEE, 1943. Training films were produced by the Technical Service Division with the cooperation of the U.S. Army Signal Corps. The average film ran about 10 minutes, and depicted activities ranging from basic military training, Quartermaster supply methods, to graphic illustrations of enemy and friendly aircraft.

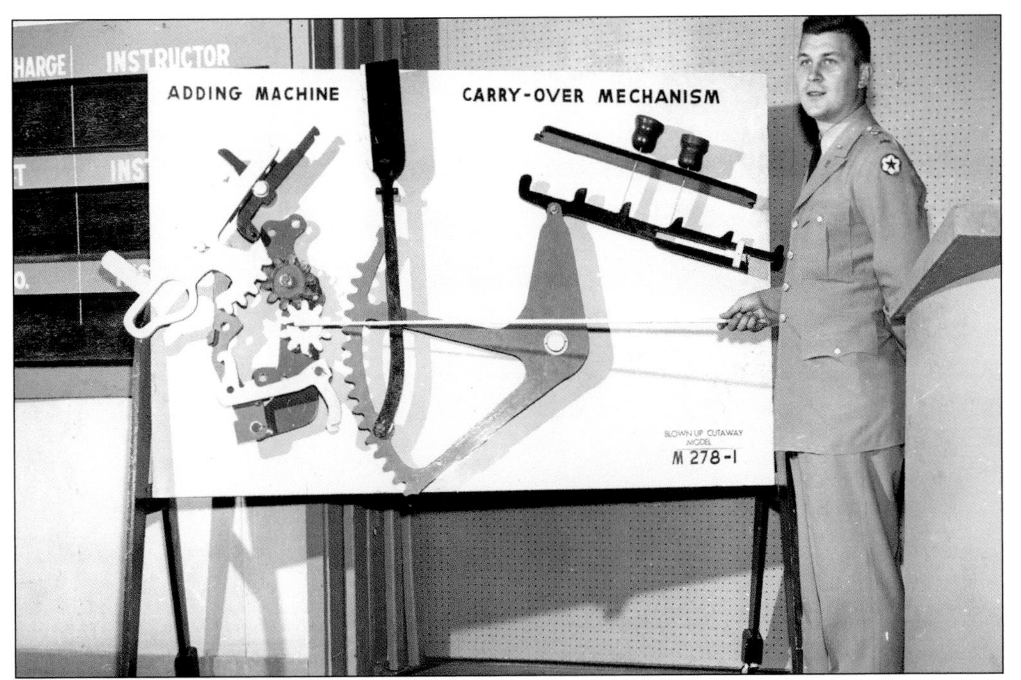

TRAINING MODELS, QUARTERMASTER SCHOOL, 1945. Models such as this, showing the inner workings of an adding machine, were used to help teach clerk specialists how to maintain office equipment.

HAND LETTERING. Trainees were taught hand lettering and other graphic arts techniques at the Painters School at Camp Lee.

NEW MATERIAL HANDLING EQUIPMENT. The widespread use of mechanical equipment—fork-lift trucks and pallets, trailers, tractors, and conveyors—was the most significant and revolutionary development in supply storage during World War II.

MODEL THEATER OF OPERATIONS. A miniature theater complete with docks, camouflaged warehouses, and model trains was used as a training aid for teaching over-the-shore logistics. It depicted a 2,000-mile fighting front telescoped into a concentrated area 250 feet long and 40 feet wide. Fifty to two hundred students sat on the ramps lining the theater as a microphoned instructor pointed out the flow of supplies from factory to foxhole.

CAMP LEE–BERLIN–TOKYO RAILROAD LINE, 1944. It never actually delivered the military vehicles and ammunition needed to "blow the Axis powers all to Hades," but the simulated train line gave Quartermaster School students a practical idea of how supplies were to be moved by rail.

DUMMY BOXCAR. Students attending the Basic and Advanced Supply Officers Course watch as seasoned experts demonstrate how to load and unload military train cars.

MOCK-UP OF C-47 PLANE. On Armistice Day 1942 the Quartermaster School christened its latest training aid—a mock C-47 cargo plane, with a 5,000-pound load capacity. Students observed proper methods of load distribution and how to lash such items as 55-gallon gasoline drums, ammo, tires, crates, and bales.

MATERIALS HANDLING EQUIPMENT TEST AREA. Students taking the Quartermaster School warehousing course learned to drive four-wheel tractors and forklifts, and to skillfully operate a range of new materials handling equipment.

QUARTERMASTER BOARD FIELD TESTING AND EVALUATION COURSE, CAMP LEE. In 1942 the Quartermaster Corps's research and development division constructed a field training site at Camp Lee to test new items of food, clothing, and equipment. Here soldiers are crawling through the mud, in the "Dynamic Rain Course," testing the adequacy of foul weather garments and equipment.

SATURDAY MORNING INSPECTION. During "Commandant's Time," the Commander himself might conduct routine inspections to get a sense of how training was going. Here he would be looking for a tight bunk, uniforms properly hung ("dress right dress"), shoes lined squarely under the bed, and footlockers properly displayed with rolled socks, shaving implements placed just so, and all other items clean and in their designated spots.

OFFICER CANDIDATES STUDYING MILITARY LAW. Many courses at the Quartermaster School retained the standard lecture/discussion format. But as the war progressed, instructional techniques bent much more heavily toward small group conferences, field demonstrations, and hands-on training.

A Swearing-in Ceremony at Whittaker Dell (amphitheater), Camp Lee, 1942. During the course of World War II nearly 25,000 soldiers graduated from Quartermaster Officer Candidate School and were commissioned as second lieutenants. In the last five months of 1942 each class averaged over 1,000 students.

Passing in Review, OCS Graduation Ceremony, 1943. There was a crushing need for Quartermaster officers in the months immediately following Pearl Harbor. So critical was that need that in 1942 two entire OCS classes with a combined enrollment of more than 2,400 candidates were commissioned two weeks ahead of their proposed graduation date, after only 11 weeks of training.

Officer of the Day Poses with WACs at Camp Lee, 1944. Both enlisted and female officer soldiers began arriving at Camp Lee in mid-1942. A Women's Army Auxiliary Corps detachment was activated at the Quartermaster School in June 1943. By 1944 there were nearly 200 WAC Quartermasters assigned to Camp Lee.

Bull Session. The caption accompanying the photograph below reads, "Members of the 47th WAAC Post Headquarters Company find there's nothing like a nice, friendly 'bull session' prior to reporting to work in the morning."

Officer Candidates Leaving Class at the End of the Day. After Pearl Harbor, the emphasis was on training would-be officers in a field-type setting, and using "hands-on" techniques as much as possible. But that still left many hours for pouring over military texts and listening to classroom lectures.

Camp Lee Soldiers Visit Petersburg National Battlefield, 1941. In their off-duty hours, soldiers at the Quartermaster Replacement Training Center got a chance to visit many historic sites in the Richmond-Petersburg area, including the Civil War battle of the Crater.

FORT LEE OFFICERS CLUB, 1945. Built in 1942, the Officers Club features a large ballroom on the main floor, other dining areas, special meeting rooms on the first and second floors, and bars and recreations facilities in the basement. Two oversized murals of Generals Washington and Lee and their staff hang above the fireplaces on each end of the main ballroom. Flags of all the Allied nations in World War II lined a circular drive in front of the building, and behind was an Olympic-size swimming pool.

"ALL WORK AND NO PLAY IS TABOO AT CAMP LEE." Wartime trainees had ample opportunity to socialize. Movie theaters, post exchanges, regimental recreation halls, and service clubs were often filled to capacity during off-duty hours. On designated nights groups of volunteer "lovelies" from surrounding towns came on post to participate in dances, socials, and games.

Camp Lee Travellers Baseball Team. Inter-service athletics played a key role in sustaining soldier morale at Camp Lee. The post fielded professional level teams in baseball, football, track, and boxing. Also offered were organized intramural leagues for horseshoe, volleyball, push-ball, swimming, and table tennis.

After-hours Drink at the Officers Club, 1944. The Quartermaster School had its own Officers Club at the far end of post where they could meet and relax during off-duty hours. The school crest displayed above the fireplace carries the motto "*Famam Extendimus Factis*—We Spread Our Fame By Our Deeds."

GUY GIBBEE VISITS REGIONAL HOSPITAL, 1944. Guy Gibbee, the well-known 1930s and 1940s character actor and star of stage, screen, and radio, here gives a live performance to patients in the Post Hospital. He is said to be discussing "politics and women" with the boys—much to their amusement. Mr. Gibbee's son graduated from Quartermaster Officer Candidate School at Camp Lee.

ARNO BENNETT, POPULAR CLUB ENTERTAINER. Mr. Bennett also sang for the patients at the Camp Lee Regional Hospital as a member of the Guy Kibbee USO Camp Show.

AUTOGRAPHED PICTURES FOR OUR BRAVE TROOPS. Famous screen actress Ann Sheridan, whose many films included the 1942 hit *King's Row*, co-starring Ronald Reagan, sent this picture "To the Fighting Q.M. Corps" at Camp Lee.

LAKE JORDAN PAVILION, 1944. The Quartermaster Association purchased Lake Jordan nine miles south of Petersburg, Virginia, along with 200 wooded acres surrounding it, for both training and recreational purposes. Here a group of officers are shown passing out cigars after dinner.

QUARTERMASTER SCHOOL CELEBRATES ITS SECOND ANNIVERSARY. October 1944 marked the second year following the Q.M School's removal from Philadelphia to Camp Lee. The new Post Commander, Brig. Gen. George A. Horkan (left) is joined by an unidentified officer for the cake-cutting ceremony.

BLACK SOLDIERS AND FAMILIES AT CAMP LEE, 1944. Thousands of black soldiers lived and trained at Camp Lee during World War II. And, as in the past, they were largely confined to segregated units and "Jim Crow" rules for off-post transportation. However, the Post Commander, Brig. Gen. George Horkan (shown in both photographs) received recognition in the halls of Congress for the sensitivity and creativity he showed in setting up an integrated bus line running from nearby Petersburg to Camp Lee.

HOMELESS CHILDREN WIN CAMP LEE NATIONAL ATTENTION. Pvt. Louis Price of Philadelphia (left) hitchhiked to camp with his three children in tow, their mother having been hospitalized. Local nurses (below) "adopted" the three-year-old twins and their nine-year-old sister for several days, until social services found them real homes back in the Quaker City. In the meantime this human interest story caught the attention of major newspapers from coast to coast.

QUARTERMASTER SCHOOL CHAPEL FOR THE SOLDIERS' SPIRITUAL COMFORT. This was one of several wooden chapels built at Camp Lee during World War II. It was modern in every respect, and even had electric chimes, which were exact replicas of the chimes at the Annapolis Naval Academy Chapel. The school chapel was regularly attended by soldiers of the Catholic, Protestant, and Jewish faiths.

CHAPEL WEDDING, CAMP LEE, 1943. Another happy wartime bride and groom are joined in this traditional military wedding ceremony.

CAMP LEE PRISONER OF WAR CAMP, 1944. Nearly a 1000 German POWs made Camp Lee their home in the last year of the war. The first arrived in February 1944 from North Africa, Sicily, and Italy. Many more came in the late summer following the Normandy campaign. They were well treated and were judged hardworking and exceedingly cooperative—except for a few "arrogant NCOs" and some "extreme pro-Nazi privates" who staged a sit-down strike on Hitler's birthday, as noted in an official report at the time.

MILITARY POLICE DETACHMENT, CAMP LEE, 1943. A "city" the size of Camp Lee needed a well-disciplined and highly trained force to maintain security and good order—the job performed by the local MP Detachment.

"EYES RIGHT!" Yet another group of soldier-technicians, having just graduated from the Quartermaster School, render a final salute as they depart Camp Lee enroute to the Pacific in the final months of the war.

TECHNICAL AND TACTICAL EXPERTISE TAUGHT HERE. In the "Administrative Laboratory" (above), a group of Quartermaster students from the Basic Enlisted Administration Course apply their knowledge under simulated conditions. At right a group of trainees learn the fundamentals of rifle marksmanship before going out to the range for "jawbone" practice and record firing.

CAMP LEE HEADQUARTERS BUILDING, 1944. The Commander and his staff (here posing in front of the Post Headquarters) were justifiably proud of the role the Quartermaster Replacement Training Center, school, and installation had played throughout the war by turning out tens of thousands of well-trained logistics soldiers.

CAMP LEE DEMOBILIZATION, 1945. By the late summer and early fall of 1945 Camp Lee, like other major posts, was making every effort to facilitate the demobilization process. The war's end meant it was time to "bring the boys home."

Four

From a Camp to a Fort

Fort Lee Main Gate, 1959. During World War II, Camp Lee served as the Army's Quartermaster Training Center but unlike after World War I, remained operational after the war. In April 1950, the Army elected to grant Camp Lee permanence by renaming it Fort Lee, recognizing the importance of professionally-trained logisticians to the battlefield success of the Army.

WAC RECRUITS RECEIVING SHOE FITTINGS, 1950. In 1948, the Women's Army Corps (WAC) Training Center was established at Camp Lee. The WAC had served with distinction and commitment in World War II, convincing the Army's leadership of the importance of women serving in the Army. In 1948, the Women's Armed Services Integration Act was signed into law, effectively integrating women into the Armed Forces. The WAC Training Center continued at Fort Lee from 1948 to 1954, until it was moved to its new home at Fort McClellan, Alabama.

WAC PHYSICAL TRAINING, 1951. Under the supervision of Second Lt. Kathryn Brown, WAC trainees undergo physical training at the WAC Training Center.

WAC GRADUATES, 1950. The WAC Training Center provided basic soldier training and Army orientation for both enlisted and officer WACs. These WACs have completed their basic training and are departing for advanced occupational training given at other schools such as the Signal Corps, Transportation, and Adjutant General's Schools. Those WACs who enlisted for Quartermaster skills remained at Fort Lee for advanced training.

SOLDIERS ARRIVING AT FORT LEE TO BEGIN TRAINING, 1950. When the Korean War erupted in June 1950, the training load at Fort Lee quickly accelerated to meet the sudden need for logistical support personnel in the far east. The population of the Quartermaster School continued to grow at a rapid pace throughout 1951–1952.

BUNK INSPECTION, 1949. Major General Horkan, now the Quartermaster General, conducts a bunk inspection of ROTC Cadets. From 1944 to 1945, Maj. Gen. Horkan had served as the Quartermaster School Commandant and Post Commander.

WET WEATHER CLOTHING TEST, 1951. The Quartermaster Board Testing Agency, established at Fort Lee during World War II, was responsible for testing uniforms and equipment prior to being issued to the Army. These soldiers assigned to the board are testing wet-weather clothing on a course that has three-inches-per-hour "rain" with rugged wear conditions. The Korean War accelerated the testing of clothing and equipment needed for the cold Korean winters.

BOOT TESTING, 1951. New footwear was tested at the shoe course at the Quartermaster Testing Agency. An inspector checks the wear on rubber boots after being put through a series of tests.

PARACHUTE RIGGERS, 1950S. The Aerial Supply and parachute rigging mission for the Army became a Quartermaster responsibility in 1950. In May 1951, the first Rigger School was established at Fort Lee. Beginning with the Korean War, Quartermasters have rigged supplies and personnel chutes for the Army. Rigger trainees above and below are learning the skills to "Be Sure Always", the motto of the rigging fraternity. Before graduating each student is required to jump with the parachute that they have packed themselves.

FOOD SERVICE TRAINING, 1953. Quartermaster cooks were historically trained at Army cooking schools around the country, but by the end of World War II instruction was becoming centralized at Fort Lee. Here soldiers were trained to cook in both garrison mess-hall kitchens (above) and field kitchens (below).

EMERGENCY MASS FEEDING CONFERENCE, 1953. Maj. Gen. Kester Hastings, Deputy Quartermaster General, advises a representative of the Catholic Charities on the proper way to make cornbread on an improvised outdoor oven. Such emergency field feeding courses were a common offering during the Cold War and attracted local groups including the Red Cross and scouting organizations.

WAC COOK TRAINEES, 1952. Quartermaster Cooking Classes included WAC trainees. WAC Corporal Oneta Downey (left) and PFC Bonnie Liby (right) prepare ingredients in a GI mixing bowl.

MODEL MAKERS, 1950S. Training aids developed by the Quartermaster Technical Service Department also included models such as these miniature storage tents (above) used to teach depot organization (below).

PHOTOGRAPHIC TRAINING SUPPORT, 1951. The Quartermaster Training Center included a number of training support branches with photography and television studio capability. WAC Private Alice Grobe (above) works in the Quartermaster Technical Training Service photograph lab.

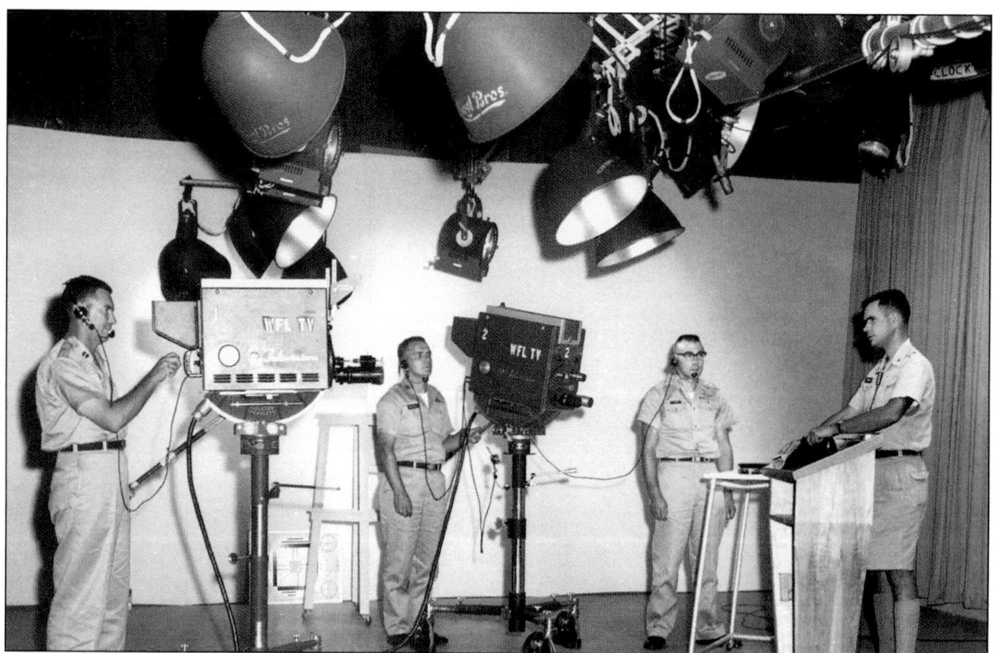

TELEVISED TEACHING, 1960S. An instructor teaches via telecast to a remote class of Quartermaster students. Television provided the means to reach classes removed from Fort Lee, a method that today continues to provide "Distance Learning" to Quartermasters around the world.

TECHNICAL LIBRARY, 1950S. The Quartermaster School Technical Library originated in 1942 to provide research materials for Quartermaster students. The Technical Library survived into the 1990s when it was consolidated with the Army Logistics Management College (ALMC) library.

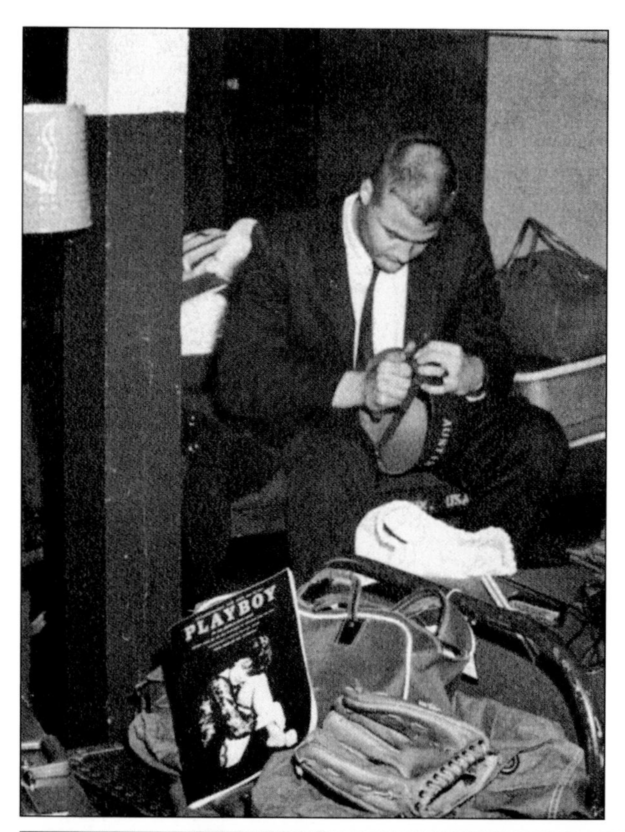

ROTC Summer Camp, 1950s. From the 1940s through the 1960s, young officers who entered the Army through the Reserve Officer Training Corps offered by colleges and universities underwent summer training in preparation for entering the active army. From their arrival (left) to physical training (below), aspiring officers learned the basics of becoming a leader in the Army.

ROTC Camp, 1950s. Officers who were selected for the Quartermaster Branch arrived from such institutions as the Massachusetts Institute of Technology, University of Texas, Purdue, and the University of Alabama for training at Fort Lee. The rigorous six-week summer program was filled with class work, field exercises, and inspections (right); but also made time for more light-hearted fare, such as tours to Williamsburg, movies, and dances at the Officers Club (above).

KITCHEN INSPECTION, 1966. Maj. Gen. Victor J. MacLaughlin, Commander of the Quartermaster Center and School, inspects one of the post mess halls on Thanksgiving Day, 1966. The MacLaughlin Fitness Center is today named in honor of Maj. Gen. MacLaughlin, who commanded the post from 1966 to 1969.

GREEN BAY PACKERS FOOTBALL STAR, WILLIE DAVIS, VISITING QUARTERMASTER COOKS, 1967. Occasional visits by celebrities go a long way to motivate soldiers in training. During the Vietnam War, a variety of well-known athletes made an appearance at Fort Lee to bolster soldier morale including Football Hall of Fame member Willie Davis.

TRAINING MODELS OF HOUSEFLY AND COCKROACH. A soldier and an airman being trained in mess hall operations receive graphic lessons in kitchen sanitation by the use of large insect models.

PIPEMAN. The "mascot" of the Petroleum Training Department, Pipeman (also known as "Pipeline Pete"), is made from pipeline sections, connectors, and nozzles. Soldiers in this department receive hundreds of hours of hands-on training in petroleum distribution and operations.

FUELING OPERATIONS TRAINING, 1969. Quartermaster petroleum training was relocated from Caven Point, New Jersey, to Fort Lee in 1954. In the years following, the course of instruction has included aircraft refueling (above) and the use of a variety of fuel sources such as the gasoline rail car (below).

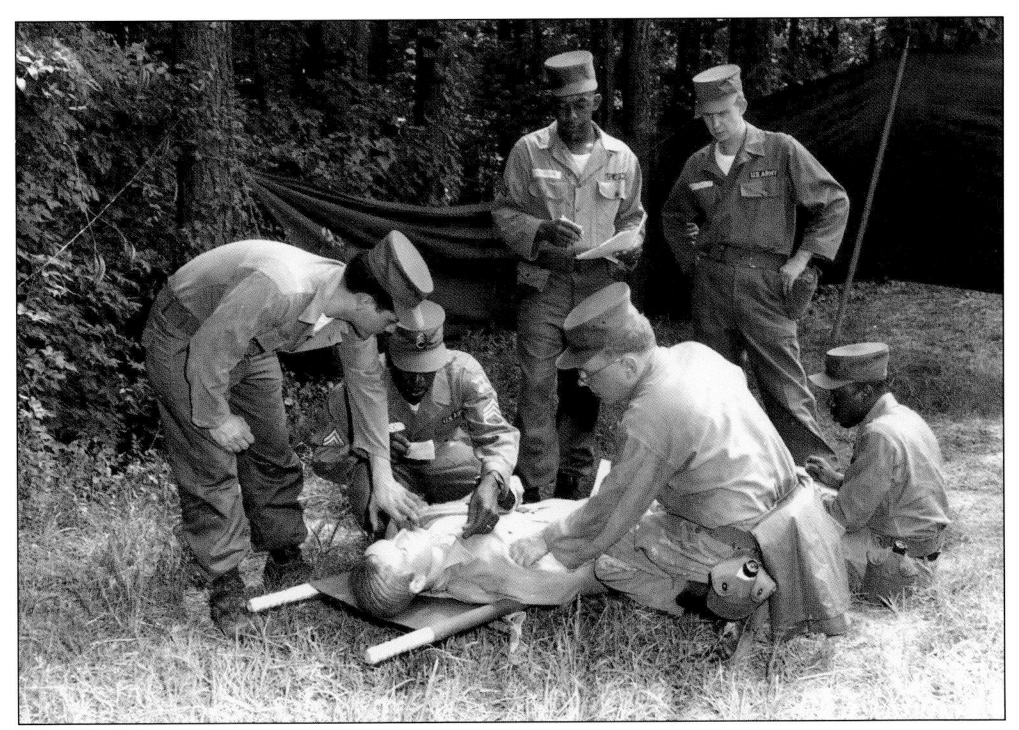

GRAVES REGISTRATION TRAINING, 1960S. Using a mannequin (above), these Quartermaster Graves Registration trainees are learning identification and removal procedures. Below, trainees learn the proper way to perform burial ceremonies in the field.

MAJ. GEN. ALFRED DENNISTON, 1960. Maj. Gen. Denniston, Commander of the Quartermaster School from 1959 to 1962, was an avid sportsman and supporter of athletics on Fort Lee. Through his influence, sports became important to soldier training at Fort Lee.

FORT LEE TRAVELLERS BASKETBALL TEAM, 1962. Fort Lee sports teams achieved near-professional status and played throughout the United States representing their installations. Second Lt. David O. Lee (left), a member of the Fort Lee Travellers Basketball Team in the early 1960s, played center and later went on to complete a career as a Quartermaster Officer, retiring at the rank of Lieutenant Colonel.

HEADQUARTERS, QUARTERMASTER SCHOOL AS IT APPEARED IN 1950. Built in 1941, the Quartermaster School retained its general appearance throughout the 1950s. The School gradually expanded as new training was offered and the space requirements soon made the original buildings obsolete.

THE QUARTERMASTER SCHOOL, MIFFLIN HALL, 1961. In 1961, the Quartermaster School received a major facelift when Mifflin Hall was built. Named after the first Quartermaster General, Thomas Mifflin, the building contained classrooms, multi-media rooms, a library, cafeteria, bookstore, and the administrative offices of the school. It remains in use today as the Quartermaster School Headquarters Building.

WASHINGTON AREA AIR DEFENSE SECTOR, 1962. In 1959, at the height of the Cold War, Fort Lee served as a location for a component of the Washington Air Defense Sector called the Semi-Automatic Ground Environment, or SAGE. SAGE was a data gathering station designed to analyze radar data from a variety of sources and plot a defense. The system was composed of two massive computers, each containing 50,000 electronic tubes. The computers were housed in a four-story building made of 18-inch blast resistant reinforced concrete that contained its own power generators and was designed to withstand direct hits. Today, the building is called simply the "blockhouse," and is used for administrative offices. The aerial view (above) taken in 1962 also shows the location of the WAC Training Center (foreground).

POST THEATER, 1948. The Post Theater was the first permanent building built on Fort Lee. It remains in use today as a theater.

NURSES QUARTERS, 1962. Nurses stationed at Kenner Army Hospital were assigned living quarters in these apartment-style buildings.

ENLISTED HOUSING, 1962. Unmarried enlisted soldiers assigned at Fort Lee were housed in dormitory-style barracks (above) while enlisted married families were eligible for family housing (below).

THE "NEW" MAIN GATE, 1962. In the early 1960s, the Jackson Circle housing area was built directly across from the main post. Its location proved inconvenient to enter Fort Lee directly and impeded the traffic on Highway 36. The entrance was adjusted to allow straight-on entry. The original entrance road is marked by the tree line on the right.

FORT LEE COMMISSARY, 1970S. From 1948 until 1979, the Fort Lee Commissary was located in this building. It served the families stationed at Fort Lee and all retirees in the surrounding area.

BASIC SUPPLY COURSE, 1960S. An instructor uses a model to demonstrate the organization of a theater of operations to an Officer Basic Class.

SUPPLY AUTOMATION CLASS, 1966. Officers in the basic supply course train on computers in an automated assisted logistics course. By the 1960s, inventory control was greatly assisted by the use of computers.

Historical Collection, 1955. One aspect of Quartermaster training begun in the 1950s was the use of history and historical artifacts to teach the evolution of Army equipment. The historical collection assembled at the Quartermaster School led to the eventual establishment of the Quartermaster Museum.

United States Army Quartermaster Museum, 1960s View. In 1962, a building was constructed for the museum, making it at that time the first structure on any Army post specifically built for use as a museum. With a collection of over 23,000 artifacts and more than 50,000 archival records, the museum continues to support soldier training at Fort Lee.

OFFICER CANDIDATE SCHOOL (OCS) CANDIDATES, 1960S. During the Vietnam buildup the Quartermaster School reopened its Officer Candidate School for the first time since World War II. Nearly 2,000 newly commissioned Quartermaster second lieutenants graduated from OCS between 1966 and 1968. These students either applied to OCS directly before coming into the Army or had been selected from enlisted applicants already in the Army.

OCS STUDENTS RECEIVE BUFFER TRAINING, 1960S. Once commissioned, these future officers delegated menial types of jobs; but while in school, OCS candidates were not exempt from GI tasks.

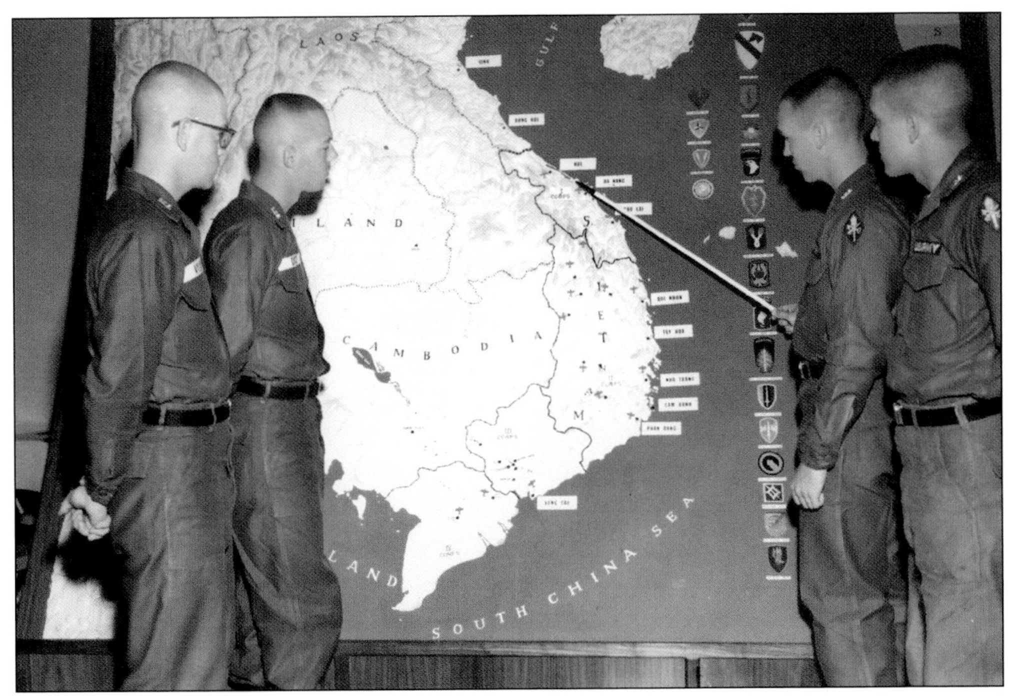

OCS VIETNAM ORIENTATION, 1967. Most of the young officer candidates who received Quartermaster training eventually were assigned to Vietnam and a large part of their training was oriented towards that prospect (above). Below, OCS students are given instruction on automated supply procedures.

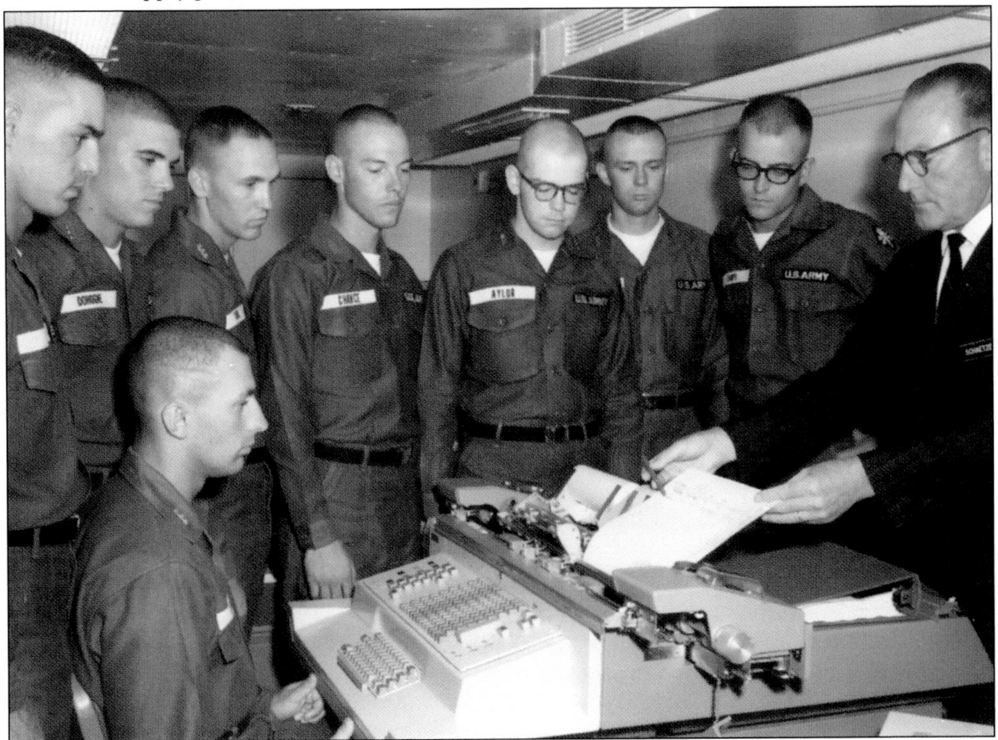

DAK BO, A MOCK SOUTH VIETNAMESE VILLAGE, 1968. As part of the expanded training for the Vietnam War, Quartermaster soldiers received familiarization training at a mock Vietnamese village under the instruction of training personnel from the Overseas Replacement Training Detachment. Above, soldiers storm the compound of "Dak Bo" and below, receive training on the hazards of booby traps, including pungie sticks.

LAUNDRY AND BATH TRAINING, 1974. Quartermaster Laundry and Bath Specialist Pvt. Shirley Christ trains on the eight-shower-head bath unit. Quartermaster missions include providing field laundry and bath facilities for soldiers living in field conditions.

FIELD BAKING. In 1976, PFC Sandra Barnes was training to be a Quartermaster Cook and was learning in a field kitchen. Between 1973 and 1978 members of the Women's Army Corps were gradually being fully integrated into military occupational skills throughout the Army, including the Quartermaster Corps.

First Logistics Command Memorial, 1974. The 1st Logistics Command was activated in 1965 in Saigon for the purpose of providing logistical support to the Army in Vietnam. Hundreds of logistics soldiers lost their lives during the Vietnam War and in 1974, veterans of the command raised the funds to erect a memorial for those killed. The memorial was rededicated in 1992 to honor all logistics warriors killed in the service of their country in all our nation's wars.

Sergeant Seay Field Dedication, 1971. In 1971, the parade field in front of Mifflin Hall was named Seay Field in honor of Sgt. William W. Seay, a Transportation Corps soldier killed in Vietnam who was posthumously awarded the Medal of Honor. Seay's mother and brother, above, accompanied by Maj. Gen. John D. McLaughlin, dedicated the commemorative marker placed on the field.

BICENTENNIAL COMMEMORATION OPENING CEREMONY, JUNE 14, 1975. Fort Lee's celebration of the nation's, and the Army's, 200th birthday began in front of Mifflin Hall, named after the Army's first Quartermaster General. Maj. Gen. Dean Van Lydegraph, the Quartermaster School Commander, hosted the four-day event that included proclamations, reenactments, balls, and dedications. Below, one of the reenactment groups is shown marching onto Seay Field as part of the ceremony.

BICENTENNIAL BALL, JUNE 1975. Major General and Mrs. Van Lydegraph, dressed as "General and Mrs. Thomas Mifflin," the first Quartermaster General, cut the cake at the Quartermaster Bicentennial Ball.

HORKAN HALL DEDICATION, JUNE 1975. Pictured here is Major General Van Lydegraph, accompanied by Mrs. Horkan, dedicating Horkan Hall. General Horkan commanded Fort Lee in World War II and later served as the Quartermaster General. Mr. Bob Davis, wearing the uniform of a 19th Century Post Quartermaster Sergeant, assists with the ceremony.

Five

Fort Lee in the 21st Century

Regimental Review, 2001. First Sergeants of the 240th Quartermaster Battalion, 49th Quartermaster Group, lead their soldiers during the Quartermaster Regimental Review in June 2001. At the turn of the 21st century, the Quartermaster Corps and the Army were in the midst of the transformation that would determine the nature of logistical support on future battlefields.

DEPARTING FOR DESERT SHIELD, 1990. Pictured here are soldiers from Fort Lee deployed to Southwest Asia to support operations Desert Shield and Desert Storm, including these members of the 16th Field Services Battalion, 49th Quartermaster Group. Fort Lee also served as an in-processing center for Reserve Units deployed to the war and as a site where Quartermaster units received additional training prior to departure to the Gulf.

14TH QUARTERMASTER DETACHMENT TRAINING SITE. The 14th Quartermaster Detachment, an Army Reserve water purification unit stationed in Greensburg, Pennsylvania, was mobilized for the Gulf War and underwent training at Fort Lee. On 19 February 1991, the unit arrived in Dhahran, Saudi Arabia, but six days later an Iraqi SCUD missile hit their barracks, killing 29 American soldiers and wounding 99 others. The 14th Detachment lost 19 soldiers and suffered 43 wounded. The 14th Detachment endured the most casualties, 81 percent of its total strength, than any other Allied unit during Operation Desert Storm. Memorials to the 14th Detachment are located at the United States Army Reserve Center in Greensburg, Pennsylvania, and at the 14th Quartermaster Detachment Water Training Site, Fort Lee. In 1993 a gymnasium on Fort Lee was memorialized as "Clark Fitness Center," named in honor of Specialist Beverly Sue Clark, a member of the 14th QM Detachment killed in Dhahran.

SOLDIER INSTRUCTION. Under the guidance of a Drill Sergeant, young Quartermaster students fresh from Basic Training are introduced to Fort Lee and the Quartermaster Center and School. Soldiers who enlisted for Quartermaster jobs, including automated supply, food service management, petroleum fueling operations, water purification, mortuary affairs, aerial delivery skills, and field service operations receive their training before being assigned to Army combat and support units.

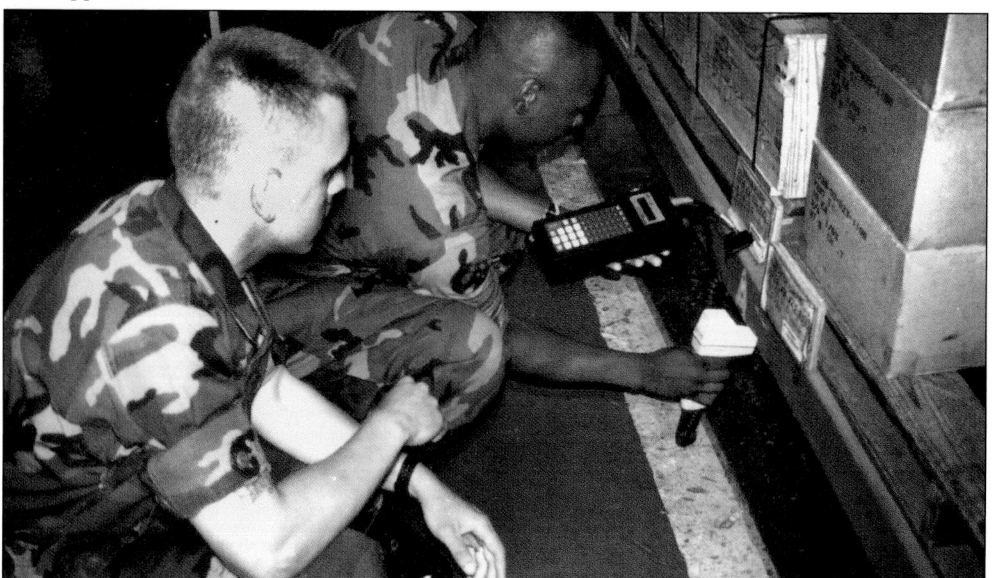

AUTOMATED SUPPLY TRAINING, 1998. The procurement, storage, and issuing of supplies to the Army have been Quartermaster missions since 1775. Issues involving distribution, inventory control, and supply tracking are being made easier through automated methods such as the bar code scanning system these soldiers trained on in the late 1990s.

FIELD BAKERY TRAINING. Food service soldiers (right) learn bread baking in the field using mobile bake ovens. In 1994, the last Quartermaster field baking units were deactivated, thus ending a service that had been offered since the American Revolution. Today, food service specialists like these shown below still learn how to make pastry products for hungry soldiers.

FIELD FEEDING. Quartermaster Food Service Specialists are trained to quickly set up mobile kitchen trailers and serve freshly prepared meals to troops in the field, even under the most adverse conditions.

UNITED STATES ARMY CULINARY ARTS TEAM, 2000. Every four years, since 1976, Army chefs from Fort Lee have competed in the "World Culinary Olympics" held in Germany. It is an opportunity for these culinary arts specialists to broaden and sharpen their cooking skills by going head to head against other major armies from around the world. The year 2000 team (above) surpassed all previous efforts by winning a total of 22 gold medals.

FIELD SHOWER TRAINING, 1998. Trainees assemble a field shower as part of their field services training. Beginning in World War I, Quartermasters have provided field laundry and bath services for the Army, a service that provides both health and morale benefits for soldiers in the field. Today, soldiers in the field are afforded a variety of comforts designed to minimize the hardships of field service.

FABRIC REPAIR SPECIALISTS, 1999. Field Services, which today include field laundry and bath services for soldiers on deployment, also include the repair of tents and other canvas materials. These students are training to repair heavy canvas and strapping materials in the field.

SLING LOAD TRAINING, 1995. In addition to aerial delivery, the Quartermaster's School also provides sling load certification training. Sling loading is a specialized aerial delivery technique using helicopters to carry such supplies as rations, fuel, ammunition, and medical supplies to remote sites.

AIRBORNE QUARTERMASTERS. Quartermaster parachute riggers and aerial delivery specialists must be airborne qualified and are required to maintain their jump status. Above, Quartermaster soldiers prepare to jump from a helicopter under the watchful eye of the jumpmaster.

PETROLEUM OPERATIONS TRAINING, 1999. The Petroleum Training Department trains soldiers and Marines to perform petroleum operations including transporting, storing, and distributing fuel. The School also trains Army and Marine Corps petroleum laboratory specialists (below) and officers from all the services receive training as petroleum management officers.

Water Purification and Distribution Training, 2000. In 1983, the Army's water purification mission was given to the Quartermaster Corps. Using the reverse osmosis water purification systems developed in the 1990s, Quartermaster Water Specialists can produce potable drinking water from any water source. Soldiers, above and below, train on setting up and operating water purification and distribution stations.

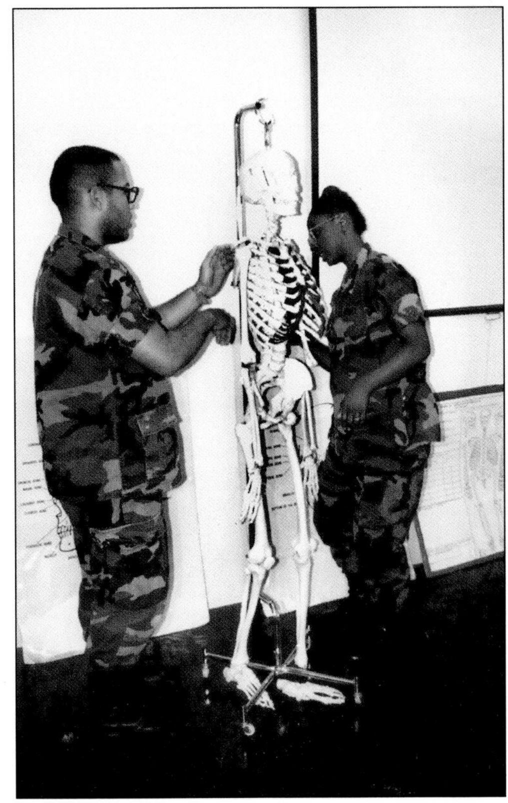

MORTUARY AFFAIRS SPECIALISTS, 1990S. Formerly called "Graves Registration," today's Quartermaster Mortuary Affairs specialists carry on the mission of recovering, identifying, and processing the remains of soldiers killed in action. Quartermasters have also assisted in other mass fatality recovery operations such as the 1995 Oklahoma City bombing and the September 11th, 2001, terrorist attacks on the World Trade Center and the Pentagon. The Army's only active duty Mortuary Affairs unit, the 54th Quartermaster Company, is headquartered at Fort Lee.

STUDENTS ATTENDING COURSES AT THE UNITED STATES ARMY LOGISTICS MANAGEMENT COLLEGE (ALMC), 2002. ALMC originated as a supply management course taught by the Quartermaster School at Fort Lee, but has evolved into a school of advanced learning for logisticians from all branches of the Armed Forces as well as international students. Accredited by the United States Department of Education, ALMC graduates over 30,000 students a year.

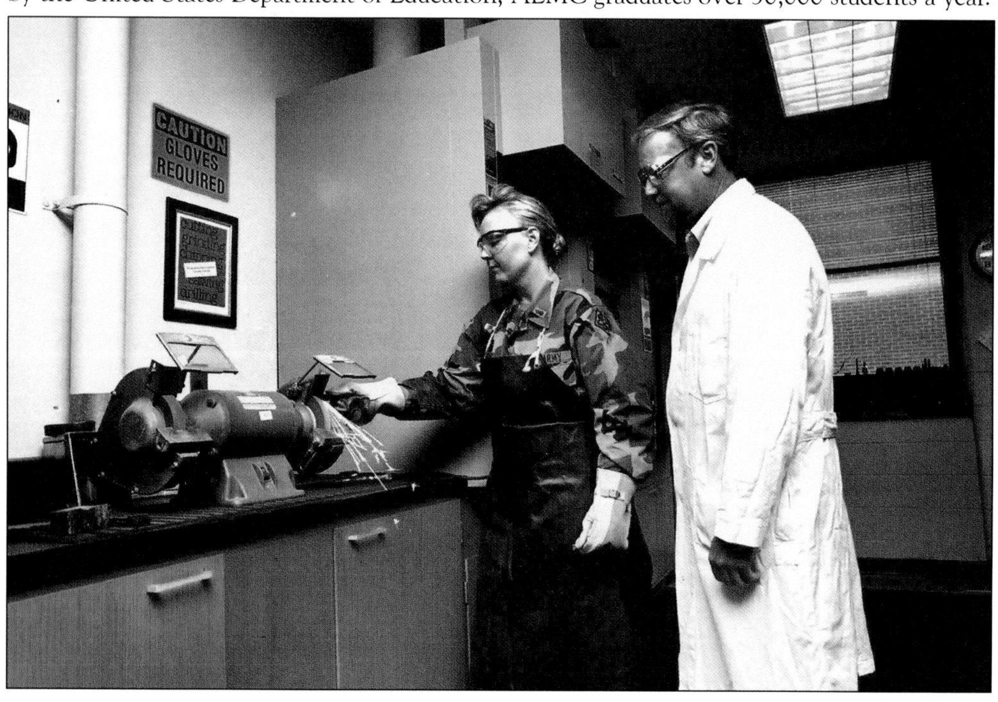

CASUALTY EVACUATION EXERCISE. Army Medical Corps personnel stationed at the Kenner Army Hospital train to respond to mass casualties. Army hospitals had been located at Fort Lee since World War I but in 1995, Kenner was reclassified as a clinic. Kenner Army Health Clinic continues to provide health services to soldiers, civilian employees at Fort Lee, and to military retirees.

FOUR GENERATIONS OF QUARTERMASTER GENERALS. During the Regimental Week 1999 hosted by Maj. Gen. James M. Wright, the 45th Quartermaster General (far right), three former Quartermaster Generals posed for a "four generations" photograph. From left to right are Lt. Gen. John J. Cusick, Maj. Gen. Robert K. Guest, and Lt. Gen. Henry T. Glisson, the 42nd, 43rd, and 44th Quartermaster Generals, respectively.

FIELD EXERCISE, 2000. Maj. Gen. Hawthorne "Pete" Proctor (above), the 46th Quartermaster General, talks with Quartermaster soldiers during their field training exercise. Quartermasters must learn how to do their jobs in the field, from running a supply distribution point to fueling vehicles, and from cooking to operating field showers.

LT. GEN., RETIRED, ANDREW T. MCNAMARA QUARTERMASTER HALL OF FAME INDUCTION, JUNE 1988. Brig. Gen. John Cusick, the 42nd Quartermaster General, presents the Hall of Fame Certificate to the 36th Quartermaster General, Lt. Gen., retired, Andrew T. McNamara. General McNamara, as a Colonel in World War II, was the First Army Quartermaster and planned Quartermaster operations for the Normandy Invasion. In 1963, he became the first Director of the Defense Logistics Agency. The Quartermaster Hall of Fame, established at Fort Lee in 1986, honors all Quartermasters who have made significant contributions to the Corps, the Army, and the nation. Only a limited number of candidates are selected each year.

ANCIENT ORDER OF SAINT MARTIN INDUCTION. Lt. Gen. (retired) Arthur Gregg, in his capacity as Honorary Colonel of the Quartermaster Regiment, presents the Ancient Order of Saint Martin to Maj. Gen. (retired) Joseph Pieklik. Induction into the Ancient Order is made only once each year and is awarded in recognition of conspicuous, long-term service to the Quartermaster Corps.

SOMERVELL HALL, COMBINED ARMS SUPPORT COMMAND AND FORT LEE HEADQUARTERS. The Combined Arms Support Command (CASCOM) is charged with coordinating logistics doctrine and developing new equipment for all logistics branches of the Army, including Quartermaster, Transportation, and Ordnance, among others. The CASCOM Commander is also the Commander of Fort Lee. The CASCOM Headquarters building is named for Lt. Gen. Brehon Somervell, the Commander of the Army Service Forces during World War II.

THE UNITED STATES ARMY WOMEN'S MUSEUM. In 1999, Fort McClellan, Alabama, the last home of the Women's Army Corps, was closed by the Department of the Army. The WAC Museum, also located at Fort McClellan, was moved to Fort Lee in recognition of the WAC's historic association with the Fort, since it was located there from 1948 to 1954. The museum, now named the Army Women's Museum, was opened in May 2001 and provides soldiers and visitors the story of women's evolution from "auxiliaries" to full-fledged members of the Army.

DEFENSE COMMISSARY AGENCY HEADQUARTERS. In 1990, the Armed Forces commissaries were consolidated into one organization called the Defense Commissary Agency, or "DeCA," with headquarters at Fort Lee. DeCA is charged with managing nearly 300 Armed Forces commissaries throughout the world for service members and their families, from procuring consumer items to building new commissaries and renovating existing ones.

FORT LEE COMMISSARY. In 1980, the new Fort Lee Commissary was built, replacing the World War II–vintage building. The 80,800-square-foot commissary provides grocery store service to active duty soldiers and their families, and retired military from all branches who live in the local area.

LOOKING TO THE FUTURE: AERIAL DELIVERY AND FIELD SERVICES DEPARTMENT TRAINING CENTER GROUNDBREAKING, SEPTEMBER 2002. Fort Lee continues to evolve both in how it trains soldiers and where it trains them. The World War II temporary buildings are almost all gone, replaced by new, state-of-the-art training facilities such as the Aerial Delivery/Field Services Department currently under construction (below). Among the dignitaries who broke ground for the new facility were, from left to right, Congressman Randy J. Forbes, from Virginia's Fourth Congressional District; Maj. Gen. Terry E. Juskowiak, the Post Commander and 47th Quartermaster General; and Col. (now Brig. Gen.) Scott G. West, the Deputy Commander of Fort Lee.

REMEMBERING THE PAST. Today's headquarters for the United States Army Quartermaster Center and School is located in Mifflin Hall (above), named in honor of the first Revolutionary War Quartermaster General, Thomas Mifflin. Fort Lee holds a special place in the memory of the thousands upon thousands of Quartermasters who trained here over the past 60 years. Among them are the men of the 58th Quartermaster Base Depot (below), who, like many other veterans, held their reunion at Fort Lee during the 50th Anniversary of World War II.

HERE'S TO THE REGIMENT! Each year in the springtime, Quartermasters young and old return to Fort Lee, "Home of the Quartermaster Regiment," to celebrate the Corps's founding during the American Revolution, more than two-and-a-quarter centuries ago. A key event in the life of Fort Lee, the annual Regimental Week involves looking to the past with pride, and to the future with confidence.